God's Special People

Ministry with the 'Handicapped'

James Mitchell-Innes
Vicar of St Peter's, Titchfield

GROVE BOOKS LIMITED
BRAMCOTE NOTTINGHAM NG9 3DS

Contents

1. Prologue 3
2. They Have Arrived 5
3. God's Image in Man and Man's Image of Man 6
4. In Church 12
5. In the Community 18

Acknowledgments

Besides my obvious debt to the authors mentioned or quoted in the text, I am grateful to the Bishop of Winchester, Rt Revd Colin James, for allowing me leave to carry out the study upon which this booklet is based. Dr Rosie Baber, Revd David Potter of Cause for Concern, Eve Gnatzy, deputy head of the special school at Ludwigsburg in Germany, Alistair Macnaughton, General Manager of Coldeast Hospital, and many others for giving me their time and sharing their experience.

Thanks, too, to my wife Carol, without whom I would never have got into this had she not had the courage to take on three children with learning difficulties as well as a husband with a dog collar and numerous other defects.

The Cover Illustration is by Peter Ashton

Copyright James Mitchell-Innes 1995

First Impression June 1995
ISSN 0144-171X
ISBN 1 85174 292 1

1
Prologue

> He grew up before the Lord like a young plant
> Whose roots are in parched ground;
> He had no beauty, no majesty to catch our eyes,
> no grace to attract us to him.
> He was despised, shunned by all,
> pain-racked and afflicted by disease; we despised him, we held him of no account,
> an object from which people turn away their eyes.

This is a fair description of a handicapped person and the reaction of society to him.[1] It is, as you will have recognized, the translation of a very ancient text but we see in it many of the difficulties encountered by the handicapped in modern society: the traumas of the early years in a hostile environment; the physical unattractiveness; society's negative reaction; the pain, mental and physical, that is often a daily part of life; the difficulty 'normal' people have in knowing how to react; being regarded as an *object* and not fully a person.[2]

The text, of course, is Isaiah 53.2-3 (taken from the Revised English Bible). It refers to the servant of the Lord and is normally taken by Christians to be a prophecy which found its complete fulfilment in Jesus Christ. If we take to heart this likeness between our Lord and the handicapped and meditate on it, allowing the logic of it to change our feeling and thinking, we will learn more than ever we will by the writing or the reading of booklets such as this. In Christ, God has drawn into himself all the weakness, suffering and failure of mankind and turned it into his glory. If we see that the cross of Christ is the great moment of God's self-revelation and his son's moment of greatest glory, then we must accept too that all that conforms to the pattern of the cross is going to be touched with the beauty of that same glory. With this understanding we will want to seek out the handicapped that they may teach us to know the Lord and that we may see him in them.

The person we call handicapped may be so in comparison to normal human physical or mental ability. But as an object of God's grace and as a visible illustration of the nature of God he is better equipped than his 'normal' brother or sister to show what it was that Jesus showed us on the cross. If the heart of God is one of

---

1　Reference to 'he' or 'she' should be taken where necessary as inclusive of both.
2　I have been using the term 'handicap' to cover people with either physical or mental difficulties or both. I have endeavoured to use the term 'learning difficulties' to speak of those who used to be referred to as 'mentally handicapped.' No term is ever going to be totally satisfactory and I have to say I find the emphasis on political correctness in the terminology used the most patronizing thing of all.

simplicity and weakness then the complete and the strong are the handicapped.

The handicapped are, along with the rest of us, actually or potentially part of Christ and included in him. This is the basic starting point of my discussion. There is nothing inconsistent between handicapped people and the life of God. The rest of what I have to say merely expands on this point in theoretical and practical directions.

I do not claim to say anything startlingly new here. It is mostly borrowed from books I have read or people I have talked to. These will be acknowledged as we go along. I am particularly fortunate in having in my family three children who would be labelled handicapped or as having learning difficulties. From time to time I shall use our experience with them to illustrate what I want to say, so I ought to introduce you to them straight away.

Terry is now approaching eighteen and then will be out of care after being with us since he was nine months old. He came to us for a variety of reasons: we wanted to express our gratitude for our own four children; we wanted to take a child who otherwise would be difficult to place; my wife is one of these people who takes children of all sorts in her stride. Terry has Down's syndrome.

Christy landed on our door step aged two and a half after a previous family found they could no longer cope and after Lisa, a little girl with Down's syndrome, had died after a few months with us. Christy came to us short term but is still with us. She has cerebral palsy, severe to moderate learning difficulties, emotional damage and recently has been diagnosed as suffering from a form of autism. She is now twelve and doing well—but drives us mad.

Aaron also came short term because he was not supposed to live more than a few months. He had heart problems which often come with Down's syndrome. He is now six, studying at the local primary school and loving life. This is only because a lot of people prayed, and because we found medics who were willing to treat him as they would anyone else and operate on his heart.

The basic convictions of this paper are the thoughts that these four wrought in my heart and which are loosely apprehended by my mind.

2
They have Arrived!

While on holiday in Cornwall with our family of five including Terry, four years old at the time, we were having a fish and chip supper in a café. A pregnant girl noticed Terry and remarked to her friend, in a scornful voice, 'Look, it's one of them.' Our nine year old daughter, always the protagonist, said to us in a voice easily audible throughout the Café, 'She could have one tomorrow!' We certainly need to listen to those who are handicapped or who are related to someone who is handicapped before we make judgments.

I am glad to say that attitudes have changed considerably since then. Now we find that our children are certainly tolerated and usually accepted in public places. It is clear that not everyone knows how to cope with them, though this is probably because they have not had the opportunity to learn.

Defective?

This is very different from my first contact with people with severe learning difficulties some thirty years ago. I worked for a few months in what was then know as an MD Hospital—a hospital for those who were mentally defective. It was a shattering experience. The wards were large, smelly and noisy with many patients confined to their beds all day. The staff seemed to keep away from them as much as possible and delegated their care to the MD equivalent of trusties. These were the more able patients and they did much of the cleaning of the incontinent, the feeding and, what I can only call as an ex-farmer, the mucking out. I had to stick close to the Lord to survive emotionally. I realize, looking back, that I should have made a fuss in the right quarters so as to try and ameliorate the conditions under which those people had to live. I did not, but a seed was planted.

At Home

Fostering or adoption is one thing that many people can do and certainly something that Christians should be encouraged to consider—since we ourselves are adopted (Eph 1.5). However, with the Care in the Community policy pressing ahead we have a more urgent and ready sphere of service to handicapped people right in our parishes. In a survey of churches in the diocese of Winchester it was found that 82% of congregations have handicapped members and 66% of those have learning difficulties. 76% of respondents were aware of other handicapped people living in their parishes. (For summary of survey results, see appendix 1.)

The impression was of ones and twos in most congregations but a few churches having much larger numbers. This survey was made in 1991 and the placing of people who were formerly looked after in the big hospitals in the community has continued apace since then. Here is a new aspect of ministry crying out for our attention.

3
God's Image in Man and Man's Image of Man

Cabbages or Kings?

'No more than a cabbage,' is one of the things people say about those who have serious learning difficulties. 'What kind of a life is that?' someone else will say, implying that the prospects of the person they are referring to do not justify their existence. I do not intend to go deep into discussion of what makes a human being distinctly human and different from the rest of creation, although the question is basic for any consideration of the care of the handicapped. If the mentally handicapped individual is not properly human there is no need to go further. It could be put down like a sick dog or a horse with a broken leg, and we need have no qualms about aborting a fetus which shows signs of handicap. If, on the other hand, we are speaking of a human being, then the same sanctity should be given to this person's life as to that of any other person. In this case we cannot justify the abortion of the fetus on the grounds of its actual or possible handicap alone for that would amount to the wanton destruction of human life as does any other abortion not carried out to save life.

Human life is not primarily about intellectual ability. No doubt the image of God in humans is made up of more than one characteristic. Intellect is one and imagination and creativity others. But I would share the view expressed by Michael Miles that, above all, sharing God's image gives the *ability to relate* to God himself and to each other.[3] This is a characteristic that is often very marked in those with learning difficulties. Some conditions involve an impairment of the ability to communicate but it is rare that it is not there at all. Indeed the desire to be with other people is often very strong in those who cannot communicate verbally or in other ways, showing that the need to relate is still very much there even if it cannot be fulfilled.

We need to add to the above the understanding of life as a pilgrimage, a process of becoming that is never complete in this life for any of us. None of us is complete in himself, only in Christ. The person with learning difficulties is certainly the equal of any of us in this. Who knows but that she has not progressed far further than you or me already. As for what she will be, that 'has not yet appeared' (1 John 3.2).

Acceptance

The person with learning difficulties, however severely affected, is a fellow human being and we must therefore accept him or her as we should any other person. 'Accept one another, then, just as Christ accepted you,' (Romans 15.7) and that means an unconditional acceptance of us as we are, as we know to our great

---

3 Michael Miles, *Christianity and the Mentally Handicapped* (CBRF, 1978).

relief and joy. We need to go further than this when we are dealing with the handicapped: when the disciples argued over who was the greatest, Jesus showed them a little child and said, 'Whoever welcomes one of these children in my name welcomes me' (Mark 9.37). Jesus is particularly concerned for those who are unable to stand up for themselves in society. The same concern is expressed in the Old Testament where God speaks of his desire that the orphan, the widow and the immigrant be especially cared for. Paul writes more than once of the importance of the 'weak' and the value of weakness. The strong are to 'bear with' the weak and he himself has learnt to 'delight in weakness' because through his powerlessness the power and life of Christ can show (Rom15.1 and 2 Cor 12.10).

Bonhoeffer says 'Every Christian community must realize that not only do the weak need the strong but the strong cannot exist without the weak. The elimination of the weak is the death of fellowship.'[4] I was privileged to visit a large, well run and well-equipped institution for handicapped people in southern Germany. The one shadow over that community was the memory of half their people being taken off to the gas chambers under the Nazi regime. 'If a society were even partially successful in eliminating retardation, how would it regard those who have become retarded?' says Hauerwas pointing out the illogic of society's position in these matters.[5] After all, not only could any couple give birth to a handicapped child but all of us, if we live long enough, will be handicapped by old age.

Ultimate Solutions

There is a principle at work behind our thinking and policy making which urgently needs to be recognized and tamed before it does even more serious damage than it already has: namely the principal of Unlimited Technological Progress or Scientific or Therapeutic Optimism (Young).

This principle tells us there will be no end to human progress and, of importance to our subject, of the ability to treat and correct handicap. This is a principle so deeply instilled into Western society that it is still heresy to question it. This is in spite of what the ecology movement is showing us of the limitations that a finite ecosystem imposes on progress. It can drive us in one of two opposite directions in our attitudes to and actions with the handicapped.

Firstly, it can tell us that we *must* do everything we can to move the handicapped nearer to being like ourselves. Thus we devise systems for treatment and education (based upon the Patterning principle) that are reminiscent of *Tom Brown's School Days* if not of mild methods of torture. Parents will do anything to gain an inch of progress from their handicapped child without considering the cost to the child itself in other areas of its life or to the family. What is the net gain or loss of spending years at the Peto Institute, for instance, when the strains on everyone are taken into account? What are the motives operating in society and, hence, in the minds of the parents, that drives both so hard in the direction of minimizing

---

4   Dietrich Bonhoeffer, *Life Together*.
5   Stanley Hauerwas, *Suffering Presence* p 163.

the handicap? I am not suggesting that nothing should be done, but that we look at why it is being done and whether it is really to the long term advantage of the person concerned. We may find that much of the efforts being made express an unwillingness to accept the person as he or she is—handicapped.

Secondly, what happens if we try and try and do not succeed? Everyone is left with a profound sense of failure and guilt. So what do we do if there is no way of 'curing' a handicap or learning difficulty or even of ameliorating it? That person becomes a living denial of the principle of Unlimited Technological Progress and, because the principle has in fact the status of religious doctrine, we must eliminate the individual. The Nazis were sufficiently convinced to be able to do this to handicapped people and those with learning difficulties who were already born. So far we have only got to the point of doing it to those who are not yet born.

We need to think carefully about consigning learning difficulties to the medical sphere. There is a danger of regarding an individual sufferer as someone who should be cured and, if there is no cure, someone who should not exist. The rapid development of genetic engineering makes this whole question one that needs urgent attention.

A recent article in the *Sunday Times* of 1st January 1995 on this subject was entitled 'Who's Playing God?' In it the authors, Sean Ryan and Lois Rogers, quote Dr Richard Roberts: 'They [politicians] try to put it on the backburner and hope it will go away, but it will not. We should use this opportunity to bring ethical issues to the fore and make people talk. Scientists have *no special claim to knowledge, insight or wisdom in this area*' (italics mine).[6]

As Christians, then, we must allow our thinking and attitude to be transformed so that we do not see handicapped people as semi-human or simply medical cases, even if (or maybe especially if) this view incites our pity. 'Labels belong on jars, not kids,' said one American mum of handicapped children. She makes a point that may seem obvious but needs to become a real part of our thinking: 'The diagnosis defines the problem, not the child.'[7] I find it difficult to accept the modern medical usage that tells me that my foster child is suffering from a syndrome which they call Down's syndrome. At least the old, discredited term, *mongol* said something about how he looks and doesn't imply that he is ill. One of the series of programmes on television entitled 'The Visit' introduced us to a family in which the two daughters were both profoundly deaf. They had been brought up entirely with hearing people for the best of reasons and never mixed with other deaf people until they were grown up. They and the parents came to see that the girls had missed something very important. They had been brought up as deaf people in a hearing world and had not, until recently, discovered what it was to live as *deaf* people in *the deaf world*.

We shall return to this when we look at the movement towards the care of handicapped people in the community but, for now, need to see that our accept-

---

[6] See Grove Ethical Study 95, Neil Messer, *Genes, Persons and God* (Nottingham: Grove Books, October 94)
[7] Bonnie Wheeler, *Challenged Parenting* p 18.

ance of the handicapped must in no way be conditional on their conforming to the ways of so-called normal society or, for that matter, Christian society. They have a contribution of their own to make and maybe a world of their own to live in which we shall only be able to know from the outside. To see Terry with his friends from special school makes me jealous of the spontaneity and open affection with which they behave towards each other. I would not want that taken away from them. That would not be acceptance even if it satisfied the demand for integration and normalization.

God's Children Too

Jean Vanier quotes the Catholic priest who was a great support to him and L'Arche in the early days of the development of their homes.:

'Père Thomas claims never to have come across a mentally handicapped person who was an atheist. "They were all believers. I will not say practising, but they were believers and they were best helped by introducing them to the Gospels and the sacraments as Jesus presented them...The first name which handicapped people respond to is not Christ or Lord, not the social functions of Jesus, but Jesus the person."'

He goes on to say,

'The basic gift of a handicapped person is that of having kept the heart of a child.'[8]

Those with learning difficulties have the same spiritual potential as anyone else. This is not affected by what may be a very low intellectual potential. Those who doubt this only need to spend time with them and introduce them to Jesus to find that it is true. In fact their 'basic gift' often gives them the advantage over the rest of us—as we might expect from the words of Jesus: 'Unless you turn around and become like children, you will never enter the Kingdom of Heaven' (Matt 18.3).

Relationship

The mentally handicapped know that people are all important. If we are to help them in the matter of their faith, we must recognize that it is *to* a person that we are introducing them and *through* a person that we will be making the introduction. Marlene Fox says, 'Often the most helpful way of integrating a handicapped child into a group is to appoint a "befriender."'[9]

Our difficulty as people with normal intellectual ability is to rid ourselves of our preconceptions and be willing to operate at the very basic level of simplicity and relationship. This requires *us* to humble ourselves and become as little children. Many will not be sure enough of the ground of their own faith in Jesus to be able to do this readily, although the person with learning difficulties may be able to teach them.

The relationship with Jesus does not require the institutional church in order

---

[8] Quoted in Kathryn Spink, *Jean Poe and Pep* (DLT).
[9] Marlene Fox *Let Love be Genuine* (BU) p 82.

to develop. But it does require the church in the form of people who will relate to those with these difficulties and, to whatever extent is possible, will relate the story of Jesus to them. The hope is that those with these special needs will be able to join with the rest of the worshipping community on Sundays and at other times. But if this is not possible two or three can gather with them and there will be the presence of Jesus ready to be appreciated in whatever ways the people concerned are capable of. As with all the ministry we perform in the name of the Lord, we must rely heavily on the Holy Spirit who will come and join us if invited. In fact this ministry is so good for us because there is nothing we can do without him, a fact of which we may not be so aware of in other circumstances.

A Special Contribution

Those of us who have been privileged to worship in a congregation alongside disabled people speak of the privilege that we enjoy and the particular contribution of the member with learning difficulties. What is this contribution?

It will depend upon the individual concerned. There is often increased spontaneity. There is simplicity not only of understanding but of life-style which contrasts with the complexity of the world most of us live in. There is an emphasis on the importance of relationships over against status or material things. Maybe the most important sermon that the impaired minds and often malformed bodies of the handicapped preach to us is that of the cross in all its miraculous foolishness and weakness.

If we say that handicap is a part of the Fall, (perhaps a result of the Fall and certainly a part of God's reaction to our fallen state) then we can see that handicap also has a place in God's way of redemption. It cannot just mean that the handicapped need to be saved and brought to the fullness of life in some particularly urgent way. But it does mean that they are material in God's hand which he can use toward the redemption of the rest of us.

For one thing, our reaction to them will show the genuineness of our faith if we are willing to go out of our way to show them the same love and acceptance that we should show to everyone. More importantly, we can see mirrored in them our own weakness and helplessness expressed in vivid physical or mental form. To accept this weakness is to embrace the cross on which the weakness of God was shown to us. We find at a deeper level the path of forgiveness and acceptance 'just as I am,' and therefore of the strength that God can give (2 Cor 12.9-10).

The handicapped test our hope—our reliance on the future that God is opening up to us and will fully open on the day of the Lord's return. We accept that, in all their deficiency, theirs is the Kingdom of Heaven and we live with them now in the yearning hope of how it will be for us together when the children of God are revealed and creation made new.

The Hope of Glory

Many of the books that I have read which are written by Christians speak of the handicapped as *God's Gifts* and *Special People*. We are especially privileged, we are told, to have the care of them and I would support this view from my own experience. They are among 'the poor' for whom the Lord has a special place in his affections and a special place in the love and affections of those whom he calls to follow him.

Does this mean that God planned for these people to be as they are, deformed and handicapped? Surely not! Surely the plan must have been for perfection in every way so that when the Lord saw what he had created he could say without reservation, 'It is good.' It must have been so in his intention for God is good and he is light and in him is no darkness at all. Deformity in the moral and physical order was not God's intention.

So, I might reason, my child is a mistake, possibly a result of the Fall but certainly not intended to be like this with clouded mind and deformed body. How then can I call this a gift from God? This person was never supposed to exist; would it not be better if she had never been born or had been helped to die? What kind of gift is this when I asked for a child to be given this caricature of humanity? What kind of loving is this that God gives me creation's mistakes—his blemished seconds? I thought he said that the he would not give me a scorpion if I asked for an egg (Luke 11.12). There is certainly a sting in the tail of this one!

I can only understand this child as a gift from God if I put out of my head these notions of perfection and set my thinking against the backdrop of the world as it is: fallen and desperate for redemption. The Saviour comes, the Saviour promised long, and see the description he takes upon himself:

> 'He had no beauty or majesty to attract us to him,
> Nothing in his appearance that we should desire him.
> He was despised and rejected by men,
> a man of sorrows and familiar with suffering.
> ...he was despised...
> ...we considered him stricken by God...
> ...he was pierced...
> ...he was crushed...' (Isaiah 53.3-5)

Within three years of his showing his colours as the Son of Man and the Saviour (see for example Luke 4.1-21) and taking up the challenge of evil, the evil had won and had him crucified and dead, lying embalmed in someone else's tomb. So it appeared—but after only three days and he is alive and evil has been made a laughing stock.

My handicapped child is another victim of evil and another *apparent* triumph for the evil one and so *destined to be another demonstration of God's redemption*. In his life, be it short or long in this world, his can be a little triumph echoing the great victory of the mighty Son of God. He is a lesser replay of the lines from Isaiah 53 quoted above and we shall see what great things the Lord will do with his little life.

Heaven

A question which often concerns the parents of people with learning difficulties is, 'What will they be like in heaven?' At the general resurrection when all of us are given our new trouble free bodies, will the handicapped be given back a handicapped body or mind? I cannot believe so. In contrast, Frances Young cannot imagine that her son will be restored in heaven because he would no longer be the boy she knows. She points us to 1 Corinthians 15—though this is a passage that for me supports the contention that the handicapped will be free of their difficulties. I cannot see how all things can be restored if the handicapped are not.

This does not mean that the value of handicap and its contribution to the fullness of the body of Christ will be lost. It will be there imprinted on the character of the remade person who is not now disabled but still bears the grace of their sufferings for the rest of us to read. In the same way the resurrected Christ bears in his hands and feet the marks of the nails and, in John's vision of heaven, appears at times as the Lamb slain before the foundation of the world as well as at others as the glorious King in triumphant robes.

This means that their contribution to the praise of eternity with loosened tongue and active mind will have all the depth of their unique experience in the same way as the martyrs are singled out for their contribution. How they will enrich our worship then as their lives do ours now!

4
In Church

Worship

Andrew used to come to church with his mother in the Dorset village of which I was then Vicar and would come up to the communion rail with the rest of the children for a blessing. It was a joy to welcome him together with the other two children with learning difficulties who lived in the village. You never knew what Andrew would come out with at any time in the service, but in particular when he was 'blessed.' 'Apples!' instead of 'Amen' was not bad, but 'Knickers' in a loud voice for all our rather respectable congregation to hear was not in the Prayer Book or even the ASB. Anyone with mentally handicapped people in their congregation will tell you of the joys but also of similar unscripted contributions to worship. Loud remarks made just as the sermon is reaching its climax, less than tuneful singing, and so on, can cause difficulties with the rest of the faithful.

But worship is important to many mentally handicapped people. Una Mennis describes the terrible tantrums her son used to have and the great unhappiness that was often evident in him. She says, 'On Sunday I took him down to church, and also took him into the empty church one weekday and said a prayer with him. He liked this; it seemed to reach him in a way that nothing else could.'[10]

Furthermore we have seen that it is important that they be a part of the church and this means entering into the main activity of the church: worship. If we understand worship rightly, it is a sacrifice offered to God and I believe it is important to God that he receives the contribution of 'these least.'

We do not need to accept any kind of behaviour from these members any more than we would from any one else. They can learn to behave in a manner appropriate to the occasion. Jonathan has severe difficulties but behaves impeccably in our services thanks to the long training he has been given by his parents. He joins in the singing enthusiastically, wordlessly but not completely tunelessly. His contribution is made in his own way so that in his own way he enriches the worship and ministers to the others in the Body of Christ. It is a joy to watch him.

Spontaneity is often a characteristic and in this we need to examine ourselves before we criticize these fellow Christians. Have we left too little room for spontaneity in our worship so that the Spirit will find it difficult to move whether through the handicapped or the other members of the congregation? It is interesting that a number of responses to my survey of Winchester Diocese asked who was *really* blind, deaf or 'handicapped.'

Our inability to express our feelings about God and one another has impaired our worship and is an area in which we can take courage and some tips from the handicapped. The mother of a handicapped child writes, 'God is the friend who made Coca Cola and flowers and sunrise and is with us all the time and wants us to talk to him. So we say "Thank you God," out loud, in the middle of the Cafe, and to the evident embarrassment of those who spend their Sunday mornings differently. And just in case they did not hear the first time, we shout "AMEN!"'

Having said this I must admit that it is much easier to integrate these people into less formal acts of worship such as family services. They will often enjoy the simpler songs and follow the illustrated talk. However, it is important not to deny them a full part, and especially a place at the Lord's Table. Words will be a problem for many but they will usually want to have the same books in their hands as everyone else and will soon learn the form, and, maybe, much of the content, of the services. Some explanation of the services and what happens could be valuable. It helps greatly if those who come together from a home do not sit all in a block together but, from the first, sit throughout the congregation. Otherwise the pattern can become ossified and affect the reaction of the congregation to them.

Let me give the last word on this topic to Jean Vanier, 'With our people here there are little words and a lot of body.' It is the body that provides the means of communication for many people whose minds are impaired so it is to the body we must look in the matter of worship and the whole business of conveying the life of Christ. Touch, symbol, music, even smell can speak when words are silent.

10 Una Meniss, *Special Children, Special God* p 68.

Fellowship

Most people want to be included and this is certainly true of those who are disabled in any way. But it may be hard for those who are limited in their ability to communicate or understand to take part in the church groups which are designed for those without such difficulties. A theological study group is not likely to be suitable. Other groups may be more amenable especially if the other members of the group are ready to adapt what they do to make their new members feel at home and benefit from the programme of the group. House groups may well be able to absorb the handicapped and profit from doing so.

However, it is possible for the disabled person to be accepted and allowed to be a part of the group without contributing much or benefiting much from the actual content of the meeting. So, even if the those with learning difficulties are integrated in the fellowship by being members of groups, it is important that someone makes sure that they are getting the spiritual sustenance that they need—teaching, sharing, relevant worship and so on. Two organizations exist to support fellowship groups for such people: Cause for Concern (Protestant) and Faith and Life (Roman Catholic).[11]

Baptism and Confirmation

For paedobaptists the question of whether to baptize an infant whose understanding is severely limited will probably be no problem but confirmation may be. Similarly those who normally baptize only adults may have problems. Before delineating these problems and offering solutions, I want to tell the story of Christy, our foster daughter who suffers from cerebral palsy. Christy was three before she was baptized because she did not come to us until she was over two. We were told that she would probably never walk and, if she did, it would not be for a long time. This opinion was confirmed to us by her physiotherapist during the week before her baptism. She was baptized on the Sunday and particular prayer was made for her that she would be cut off from the bad influences of the past. She walked on the Tuesday. There is power in the sacraments that should not be denied to handicapped people.

To return to the problems. There is first of all the principle of whether the slow learners are disqualified from Confirmation or Adult Baptism by their lack of understanding. I hope I have answered this question in what has already been said about the primacy of relationship in the Christian faith. There is no doubt in my mind that they are qualified, as are the rest of us, by the same principle of grace accepted by faith.

The second problem concerns understanding. John Bradford, in his booklet on preparing the handicapped for confirmation, reminds us that in the Anglican church it is laid down that, 'The minister shall present none to the bishop but such as are come to years of discretion and can say the Creed, the Lord's Prayer, and the Ten Commandments, and can also render an account of their faith ac-

---

[11] Details of some support organizations can be found in appendix 2.

cording to the said Catechism.'[12] Certainly, when Steven was confirmed in our church, he could do none of this. In fact the most he could manage in reply to the bishop's questions was a strangled 'yeahhhhhh.' Yet there was no doubt in my mind that it was right to present him and that he was a believer.

John Bradford in the booklet quoted above suggests a 'flexibly integrated' form of preparation using a 'Lay Confirmation Tutor.' It seems an excellent system where the people are available to do the job and, certainly, the emphasis on flexibility is important—for we are all different. The problem is least acute where the handicapped person has been a member of the church for a long time and has had plenty of opportunity to absorb the faith and respond to it. In the end, the answer must be that whatever can usefully be done in the way of preparation should be done. The rest can be left with a clear conscience.

A more difficult problem, especially with those that are not well known in the church, may be that of judging the readiness of the candidate particularly if he or she is unable to speak. One can use the method recommended by the Lord himself when he said, 'By their fruits you shall know them.' In fact, that is always a more reliable way of telling the genuineness of a person's faith, whatever her skill in communication. One must be careful not to be influenced by her handicap either to be too lenient or too strict. Jean Vanier writes, 'They have the right to be rotters, to have their own dark place, and the corners of envy and even hatred in their hearts. These jealousies and insecurities are part of our wounded nature. That is our reality.'[13] They are not so good as the rest of us at hiding their feelings and keeping the dark side of their nature curtained off, but at the same time they do not try to hide the working of the Spirit in their lives and, in the end, this is what we are looking for. If we switch off for a moment our beloved facility for intellectual judgment and switch on instead the Spirit's gift of discernment, we shall have the best chance of deciding whether or not this person is ready for Confirmation or Adult Baptism.

The sacrament itself, whichever of the two we are speaking of, is likely to be a very important and meaningful occasion for the special candidate, but he or she will need especially careful preparation. She will need to know exactly what she has to do, who is going to be there and where her family or friends are going to be. To make sure she is not disconcerted, it may be well for the parents or a friend to stand with her throughout. It is also important that she meets the main participants beforehand, the bishop and others, and certainly that she knows the minister who is conducting the service well.

It has been pointed out that there is a danger of the mentally impaired person making a magical interpretation of what is happening in the service and this is something to guard against. But if the sacrament is understood as an outward and visible sign of an inward and invisible reality, it is for this reality that we should look—that the person experience the living presence of the Spirit of God.

---

12 The Revd John Bradford, *Preparing the Mentally Handicapped for Confirmation* p.4.
13 Jean Vanier, *Community and Growth* p 43.

Evangelism

Many who work with the mentally handicapped are very cautious when it comes to conveying to the people they are responsible for the good news concerning Jesus Christ. They are conscious of the ease with which these people could be manipulated, and this is the last thing they want to do even if it is in what they regard as a good cause. Christians whose tradition makes them suspicious of evangelism anyway tend to be the most diffident. On the other hand, those from an evangelical tradition could be guilty of putting pressure on their wards that will produce a psychological effect but not a spiritual change.

We have to set against this the Lord's great concern that the poor, the crippled, the lame and the blind find their place in the Kingdom (Luke 14.13). We are enjoined to go out into the highways and byways and drag them in along with anyone else we can get hold of. But we must think carefully about the methods we use. The helpers in one Christian home had felt that it was enough to *live* the life and thus show the people in their care what Christ is like. However, they were beginning to question this presumption, feeling that they should offer the good news as well. To deny them this was to discriminate against them by not telling them what they would want to take any opportunity to tell other people.

So, the question is not whether we should try to evangelize these people, but, as with the winning of any group of people, what is the appropriate way of going about it. One woman working with the handicapped in her church said, 'I can never forget the *Spirit* who leads them *gently* to Christ.' Those two words that I have written in italics seem to me crucial in the evangelism of the handicapped. We have to have great respect for them as persons. 'The change of attitude from "wanting to do things for" to that of "listening to" is one that would take some time,' says Jean Vanier of the early days of his homes.[14] This is where we must start if it is our ambition to tell our friends the story of Jesus so that they may believe in him. I feel that, generally speaking, it is inappropriate to put any pressure on a mentally slow person to make a decision because so often they will do things out of a wish to please. They may end up learning a formula which they readily regurgitate but not learn to know the person who offers them life. The congregation must make sure that those with learning difficulties are thoroughly included in the fellowship, have the gospel explained in an appropriate way and are given the freedom to respond in their own time and way.

Healing

We have to come to terms with the question of healing for people with conditions that limit their ability to learn and understand. Medical people, ministers, parents, friends and relations of these people have to contend with the question of whether or not they should expect this person to be healed of their limitation by medical means or, in particular, by God in direct intervention linked to prayer.

On the one hand one can never say that God cannot do a thing and there are

---

[14] Jean Vanier quoted by Kathryn Spink in *Jean Vanier and L'Arche* p 42.

certainly instances of people with physical disabilities, if not with mental handicaps, being healed in the Bible.[15] On the other we have already discussed the place of handicapped people in the economy of God's Kingdom on earth and seen that there is a positive contribution that these people make with their particular gifts. Should we or should we not look for their healing?

Frances Young writes of her own severely handicapped son, 'I find it impossible to envisage what it would mean for him to be "healed," because what personality there is is so much part of him *as he is*, with all his limitations. Healed he would be a different person.'[16] I can identify with what she is saying when I look at the two youngsters in our family who have what they call nowadays 'Down's syndrome.' I can't imagine either of them different and even feel that we would lose something that is very important to us if they were. That is not the question, of course; it is *their* welfare and completeness that should be our concern. On these grounds we would wish handicapped people to be 'normal' because as they are they *are* limited and not able to enjoy the full and abundant life that is God's will for all of us. But then again, all of us have our limitations and find that these limitations are apt to grow as life goes on and the depredations of old age make themselves felt. We have to be content with the knowledge that we shall only be completely unencumbered by these handicaps after the general resurrection of the 'Last Day.'

So we find ourselves arguing ourselves around in a circle on this question of healing of handicaps and, in the end, have to come to the same conclusion on this matter as we do on the general question of healing, that *ultimately, in or out of this present age,* healing and wholeness is God's will and so should be something we seek for every individual. But at the same time we must acknowledge that not everyone is healed in this life.

In the case of mentally handicapped people I have not come across any instances where one could claim that total healing had taken place. But there are many in which improvements of one sort or another have been registered by those caring for the person. Cameron Pedie mentions a girl with Down's syndrome that he prayed for and subsequently was said no longer to have the condition.[17] Our own foster daughter, already mentioned, is a case in point. Her mental ability is still limited and she needs extra help at school although her reading and writing is good. Our GP has read what I have written about her and confirms that he never expected her to make the physical, intellectual or emotional progress that she has. Other parents and foster parents tell similar stories of how their children have responded to the prayer and care of a Christian fellowship.

From my experience and understanding of praying for the healing of these people I would make the following suggestions:
- That we pray for them expecting God to work in their lives and looking for

---

15 For example Luke 13.10-17. cf Luke 9.37-45 for an example of what might be taken for mental handicap these days.
16 Frances Young, *Face to Face* p 62.
17 Cameron Peddie, *The Forgotten Talent*.

physical, intellectual and/or emotional improvement.
- That we do not dictate to God what he must do but follow his leading in our praying and thank him for the improvements we do see.
- That we encourage those who care for the person we are praying for to think and pray this way too and avoid any suggestion that might add to their burden of guilt by implying that their faith or their praying is inadequate.
- That we recognize and, as far as we are in a position to do so, cater for the emotional and physical needs of the primary carers such as the parents.
- That we make the best of whatever medical facilities are available.

There is more to be said about the nature of wholeness and healing. But we must always be ready to acknowledge that handicapped people may in other ways be more whole that ourselves.

5
In the Community

Supporting Parents

I have suggested that to be entrusted with the care of a handicapped person could be regarded as a privilege and a means by which we may be drawn deeper into an understanding of God. He is the God and Father of our Lord Jesus Christ who was severely 'handicapped' by taking on himself human nature and carrying that nature, along with his divine nature, to the cross. This is *not* the way it is going to seem to parents who are told that they have given birth to, or are likely to give birth to, a child with spina bifida or cerebral palsy or one of the many syndromes that occur rarely but regularly. Still less is this so when that child has been normal up to a certain age and then, by accident or illness becomes handicapped. It is at this point that care for the parents needs to start.

A consultant working with disabled people admits, 'Professionals and especially doctors tend to focus upon the medical problems and ignore the psychological difficulties that the parents will have and do have.'[18] This consultant is a notable exception to her own statement which is, sadly, amply confirmed by the experience of many parents. We should not necessarily expect an obstetrician, house doctor or GP to know how to cope with the situation of his patient giving birth to a handicapped child. We expect our medics to be omniscient and omnicompetent—but then who is? On the other hand the parents badly need help at this point and at many others as they endeavour to bring up this child that is so

---

18 Rosie Baker. Consultant on mental Handicap, Basingstoke District.

different from what they had expected. I shall list and then look at some of the crisis points for parents: diagnosis; birth; realization; learning about the condition; finding support; respite; schooling; ageing.

(a) Diagnosis of handicap may occur before, at, or after birth. Whichever is the case the parents are going to need a lot of support merely in dealing with their emotions and reactions to the news. If the child is still *in utero* there will be the question of abortion which, if it does not occur to the parents themselves, will probably be offered or even recommended by the doctor in charge. The very offer of an abortion may be an affront to some parents who may need counsel and encouragement in their wish to go against the presumption that they will take this option. Whatever the parents feelings about abortion, once the subject has been raised there will be the need for careful discussion before a decision is made. Even if, as a Christian, one advises against abortion one must be prepared for the parents to make a different decision and to support them in this and to help them come to terms with it afterwards. Counsellors for the Life and Care organizations are trained to help people in these circumstances to come to a decision and to learn to live with it whatever it is. If they do not want abortion they will need support in dealing with the spoken or mute criticism of a society that feels that it has found a solution for handicap in this way: 'Why should citizens support the birth and care of such a child when its existence could easily have been avoided.'[19]

If abortion is not an option either because the child is already born, has become disabled later or this has been rejected as a way forward, the greatest need is to help the parents accept that they *have* a handicapped child and to *accept* that child. Parents may for years and against all the evidence deny that their child is handicapped but the sooner they can come to terms with the diagnosis the better for child and parents. However, there are deep reasons why a parent may find this acceptance of the fact of handicap hard so that the brutal, confrontational approach sometimes used is not helpful. Parents can be helped into acceptance and Christians will be doing an important service if they can aid this process.

To sympathize in the 'Oh-how-awful' manner is not helpful. It is much better to show love and acceptance for the child by reacting in the usual ways of wanting to know name, weight and so on and wanting to cuddle the baby and buy it little garments. Parents who themselves already have a handicapped child can often be the greatest help. Faith Bowers suggests, 'It may be that a Christian parent of a mentally handicapped child could be trained in counselling and then be of service to others facing up to the situation for the first time.'[20] The need is to be realistic but positive.

(b) Birth has already been largely covered under the previous point. Suffice it to say that it is very important that lots of support be given to the parents at this time

---

19 Stanley Hauerwas, *Suffering Presence* p 163.
20 Faith Bowers, *Let Love be Genuine* p 6.

and that people are there to listen to the parents as they express their feelings and come to terms with this severe upset to their hopes. Medical opinion differs as to how best to tell parents that their child is handicapped. The aim should be to minimize the shock and maximize the likelihood of the parents accepting the child. Usually a mother will instinctively bond with the baby whatever the defect, given time and positive encouragement. But there may well be pieces for the pastoral visitor to pick up.

(c) **Realization** of what this birth is going to mean to them will come gradually, maybe taking years before the parents reach a place of stability in their thinking and feeling. Again they are going to need support. They will pass though a forest of feelings and will need guidance, reassurance and prayer. Often there is an initial shock accompanied by incredulity and maybe rejection of the baby. An ongoing feeling of loss may even take the typical mourning pattern and will be reinforced every time the growing child's contemporaries pass developmental mile stones but the handicapped child does not. Dr Rossie Baker describes this as a 'Life-long bereavement.' There may be anger or guilt at having brought such a child into the world or, conversely, at failure to produce a normal child.

(d) **Learning** about the condition is going to be a very positive time and parents can be encouraged to contact support groups specific to the condition of their child and to read the growing volume of literature including biographical stories by parents who have been through the same experience.

(e) **Finding Support** will run parallel to learning. The church's fellowship will be vital. Una Menis speaking from her own experience of bringing up a handicapped boy says, 'The isolation of handicap is an ever-renewable pain.' Speaking of a roster of helpers that her local church in Chandler's Ford organized, 'It would have been very difficult for me to ask anyone personally, but to have it organized on my behalf was bliss.'[21] Support can also be found through GP, health visitor, and social workers. Bonnie Wheeler writes,

> 'Find a parent Support Group. I cannot stress this enough. At one meeting the highly trained psychologist who led our group asked what had been most helpful. We unanimously answered, "Just being able to share honestly with people who understand."'[22]

On the whole I agree with this but add a caution. Not all parents find such groups helpful and some groups may become so intense and militant that they rather serve to reinforce the parents' isolation. They may find themselves in a ghetto world of similarly placed parents.

Nursery schools provide an excellent forum for parents to meet and talk. The one my wife worked at in Winchester, the Meadcroft Opportunity Group, was

---

21 Una Menis, *Special Children, Special God* p 49.
22 Bonnie Wheeler, *Challenged Parenting*. p 29.

actually started in a church hall by church parents but now comes under the Education Service.

In the end there is no one like a friend.

(f) Respite from the never-ending demands of this kind of parenting is vital to the main carer, usually the mother but also to the whole family. In the USA four out of five marriages where there is a handicapped child fail. In this country it is two out of three and rising—twice the normal rate. Fortunate the family who have grandparents willing and able to look after the child for days and week-ends. Social services can sometimes offer help either in homes or with short term foster parents but they are always short of people to man respite schemes. Here is an area in which any church should be able to help both parents of church members and those living in the area who they are in contact with.

I should say that lack of respite is not the only reason that marriages are so vulnerable when parents are having to cope with a handicapped child . The other big factor is the emotional adjustment needed. Unless this is carried through by *both* partners the flaw is there and may easily open up into outright rift.

(g) Selecting a School is an important point for parents which may well bring to the surface unresolved feelings. If Special School is suggested, this makes public the stigma of having an abnormal child in the family. Again support and counsel is needed and there may well be battles to be fought with local education authorities whose ideas of what is best for the child differ from the parents.

A father of two children under school age, a boy of four and a little girl of nine months with Down's syndrome, used to get home from work early once a week so that his wife could do a few hours at her nursing profession. Speaking of that time with the children he said, 'That hour and a half (before they were both in bed) is more tiring than my eight hours at work and *much* more interesting.' The baby has since died and the parents are having to live through their grief. But they look back with tremendous gratitude on the time that they had with Emily and are even talking about fostering or adopting a difficult to place child later on. It is to this point of active acceptance and appreciation of their child that we need to try and help parents by our prayers, support and counsel.

School and Work

I have found very little written about the schooling of the mentally handicapped from a specifically Christian point of view, yet most parishes have active contacts between the church and main-stream schools. Incumbents spend a considerable part of their time in these schools but few are involved in Special Schools. Yet these schools are at the sharp end of the integration programme and contacts made at this stage will make it easier to integrate handicapped people in the church's life later on.

This is only one reason that the church should be involved in special education. The most important one is that we should be involved because of our Lord's particular love and concern for these people—these so *special* children.

A member of my church has been working in special education with the Church of Uganda. One of the projects she has been involved with came about through the initiative of some of the villagers of Guluddene, a village in the area worst affected by the recent war. They asked her to help them set up a school for handicapped people. This is quite a rarity in such a poor country where resources are channelled into those areas where they are likely to give the best results in terms of progress and development. When I had the opportunity to question one of the prime movers during his brief visit to England in 1990, I asked him why he and his village had decided to put their efforts and money into helping the handicapped rather than setting up a school for the other children of the village.

His reply was that Jesus always helped the handicapped—the people who could not help themselves—so they were sure that this is what Jesus would want them to do. It is revealing to set this profound response to our Lord with the situation here in England where, as far as I know, there are *no church special schools*. I believe this says something very telling about the elitist attitudes that have long governed the Church of England. We need, once again, to learn from our African friends. Maybe the day for founding a church special school is past because of the movement towards integration. But many ordained and lay church people are involved in schools, many as governors, and will be able to influence their schools when the question of integrating handicapped people into them arises. I hope the church will be able to put right its neglect of these young people now. It may have to be done at a cost, especially with local management of schools now well under way. There will be the temptation to channel resources made available to a school for special needs provision into projects of benefit to the whole school rather than directly to the costly business of educating the handicapped for life. Also, those with learning difficulties are not going to raise either the kudos of the school or the figures for its exam results. There will be great gain in having these children on the roll, but it will not be what is usually counted as gain.

If one gets involved with special schooling one will probably find that teachers have the same difficulties that their counterparts at main-stream school in satisfying the legal requirements about assemblies and religious education. This will be exacerbated by the fact that most people understand religion in terms of concepts which need to be conveyed, concepts which are very deep and involved which they do not understand properly themselves. Not many have grasped the truth that Christianity is mainly about *relationship*.

In Germany we stayed with the acting head of a special school. She showed us the RE syllabus for her school. It is over 300 pages long! She described a joint RC/Lutheran confirmation service that they had recently held in the school and the work of her *two* specialist RE teachers. We have a long way to catch up on this but we could at least make a start on using our constitutional privileges in these schools. If the incumbent feels out of depth in this kind of school, they often have wide catchment areas and there is the possibility of finding a colleague in one of the denominations who would be interested in working with the staff in developing meaningful Christian input, both of worship and teaching.

It does not have to be the priest or minister who gets involved on behalf of the church. One head of a special school said that she would welcome people coming to work voluntarily at her school as long as they were willing to operate at the appropriate level and did not bring with them preconceptions from the world of main-stream schooling. I imagine most heads would share her views. It strikes me that this kind of involvement could be of mutual benefit: not only an extra pair of hands for the school but the person concerned would be gaining experience which could then be used in the church context. It could turn out to be a very useful piece of missionary work in the widest sense for someone who was prepared to commit the time and effort to it.

As integration proceeds, we may find these children turning up in our local schools and again have the opportunity to work with them in an appropriate manner. May I say also that no one should be deterred by the feeling that this is specialist work best left to the specialist. It will not take many hours of observing the way the teachers relate to the children and how they relate to each other, before the candidate for this ministry begins to get the idea.

One of the ambitions of teachers and others who work with the handicapped is to see their pupils not only living in the community, but working there too. It is also Government policy to encourage firms to employ a proportion of handicapped people. Schools and colleges are beginning to provide work experience for their pupils with the aim of preparing those who are capable for a 'proper' job. The need is for employers willing to take on handicapped people. The church could itself be one such employer, but, more effectively, could suggest to church members in a position to help that they consider taking on handicapped people. Day centres are very well but it is still not integration and many handicapped people are capable of much more than these can offer. Furthermore, the level of funding of these places is such that they are able to offer less and less in the way of real work and supervision.

I observed an interesting difference between the philosophy of work with the mentally handicapped in Germany from that which prevails in this country which, I believe, reflects a general difference in national attitudes. In Germany work is regarded as the prime condition for a handicapped person to live a normal life. So we found a heavy emphasis on training for a job at, for instance, the Karlsohohe centre at Ludwigsbourg. Obtaining a job was seen as the end product of their very demanding training programme. 70% of the trainees (mentally and physically handicapped) get jobs. They will be required to work a full day and will be penalized for non-attendance in the same way as anyone else except if it is for health reasons. They will be paid according to their output. At the time of our visit, plans were afoot to start a company which would employ some of the remaining 30%.

In England we seem to have a more patronizing attitude, and one could not call our day centres serious work places in the way that the German equivalents are. Here there is no obligation upon employers to take on a proportion of handicapped people as there is in Germany. It is little more than a suggestion. It is encouraging to see some firms taking this up and employing disabled people but they are few. Serious preparation for working life is sparse and rudimentary.

We can see how the national practice in both cases arises out of national attitudes and the Christian position may be different from either or somewhere in between. But if we take seriously the rightness of integration and the need to accord equal dignity to the handicapped, then work is going to be as important to them as it is to other men and women. We need their contribution to the workplace and the economy and they need the dignity of making that contribution.

Care in the Community

In his report,*The Local Church and Mentally Handicapped People*, Michael Bayley comments, 'There is a steadily growing emphasis on enabling mentally handicapped people to live within the community.' He continues, 'Parallel with this there is growing realization that mentally handicapped people need as normal experience of life as possible.'

He points out the need for the churches to respond to this movement and cautions: 'Just because mentally handicapped people are living in a given locality it does not mean that they will have good contacts with that neighbourhood. Their home can all too easily become an isolated unit in the community rather than a part of the community.'[23]

It was very interesting to spend a week in southern Germany looking at two large church-run establishments caring for the handicapped in the company of a group of young Americans, working also with handicapped people in their churches. The Principal of Stetten, one of these two institutions caring for 1,000 handicapped people, strongly defended the type of care he was providing and it certainly was first class of its kind. The Americans, who are further down the road of integration than we are, regard it as a basic human right on a par with racial equality that every disabled person be integrated in normal society right through his life. The German Principal responded vigorously pointing out the disadvantages: that there would be no special facilities available; that the people concerned would be isolated; that there would be a lack of the appropriated spiritual care that was available to them at Stetten; that someone would have to create a costly network of support.

I tell you this to show that there are two sides to the debate and much will depend on the response of the community to the people concerned. Especially anxious are parents of severely handicapped people. Frances Young says, 'The dogmatic pursuit of policies of normalization is just as unsatisfactory and may be equally hurtful.'[24]

The general manager of Coldeast Hospital near Fareham had seen half his patients placed in the community in some 30 homes by 1991. When he asked

---

23 Michael Bayley, *The Local Church and Mentally Handicapped People* (CIO, 1984) paras 3,4 &6.
24 Frances Young, *Face to Face* p 173.

them whether they would like to stay in their new home or return to Coldeast, 99% said that they did not want to go back. When I asked Dr Baker about the success of the nine houses for the handicapped that she is responsible for in the Basingstoke area, she felt things were going well on the whole and that the reaction of the community was quite positive but emphasized that the locality needs to be selected with care for the suitability of its community. I spoke with a vicar from one of the less prosperous areas of the town who has a large number of mentally sick and handicapped people in his congregation as a result of the care in the community project. He felt that the churches on the estate were about the only appropriate manifestation of *the community* in his parish. This may well turn out to be the case in many, especially urban, areas, posing a problem or providing an opportunity depending on how it is viewed.

Now that the closure of the hospitals that used to cater for people with learning difficulties is well under way, the problems of community-based care are beginning to emerge and the main one, predictably, is underfunding. It was known that there would be no savings from Care in the Community if it was done properly since it costs roughly half as much again to keep someone in a small house in the community than it did to keep them in a large hospital. Funding was actually cut last year (1994) which means that levels of care will have to be lowered. We shall probably be hearing from Christian organizations running homes appealing for funds to supplement their budgets and maintain a reasonable standard of care. We shall be seeing mentally handicapped people on the streets as we do those with psychiatric illness because the homes and the Day Centres do not have the funds to look after them all day, seven days a week. Hard-pressed voluntary bodies and churches will be called upon to plug the gaps.

For an Anglican, who sees his calling as to the whole parish rather than just his congregation, there will be a desire to reach out to the handicapped whether they live at home or in 'homes.' Judging from staff I have met, any approach will be welcomed as long as it is done in a way that recognizes the integrity of the residents. The woman in charge of one Community Centre for the handicapped that I visited was herself a Christian. She longed for people who would come in the Lord's name and spend time at her centre getting to know the 'clients' and thus being in a position to invite them to church. Many privately run homes have some recognized system of people to visit and befriend. The Wallsingham homes call them 'friends,' the Guidepost homes, 'Volunteers.' Church people who take on this role not only find that the friendship is very much two way and they gain more than they give, but they may well gain disciples for their Master too.

Appendices

1. Survey of the Involvement of Churches in the Winchester Diocese with People with Handicaps.

The questionnaire was sent to all the churches of the Diocese intending that each church as distinct from each incumbent should fill in a form. This was not always understood and a number of replies represent more than one church and parish. There was also some confusion over the difference between mental handicap/learning difficulties, physical handicap and mental illness. However, sufficient replies were received in time to analyse and give a fairly reliable overall picture of the churches' involvement with mental handicap in the diocese.

113 replies were received.

1. 82% of Congregations have members who are handicapped. Almost all these have physically disabled people and some 66% those who have learning difficulties. The most common physical disability is deafness (73%). Blindness is not so common (30%).

These results show a wide spread of disability in our churches with the usual pattern being ones and twos in each congregation. The importance of the induction loop is underlined by the large numbers of deaf, often older, people.

2. 65% of churches make some kind of special provision for the handicapped, most often to do with access to the church buildings (41 provide wheel-chair access). Other special provision includes: loop system (35), disabled toilet (15), transport (13), large print books (12), special attention to the handicapped in various ways (7 churches), home communion (very common), feeding cups (1), communion by intincture (1). People with learning difficulties are mostly provided for by including them in whatever parish activities are thought to be appropriate rather than setting up special groups.

3. The majority (235) of the handicapped of all sorts live at home. 142 were said to live in 'homes' and 56 in institutions. Many respondents did not fill in numbers so these figures are not reliable.

4. 76% of respondents are aware of handicapped people other than those involved in church who live in their parishes. Of these, 63% are handicapped physically and 55% mentally.

5. Of the churches in (4) above, 64 out of a total of 80 have some involvement with these people.

6. 20 churches have schools for those with learning difficulties in their parishes (18%);13 of these are for mild learning difficulties and 8 for severe.

42% of parishes contain some other provision for handicapped people.

Of those with either schools or other provision in their parishes 84% are involved with these in some way.

The survey also enquired as to what help parishes would appreciate in their ministry to mentally handicapped people. The results are as follows.

1. 39 churches would like to know what facilities for the mentally handicapped lie within their parish boundaries.

2. 28 churches would like help in enabling their congregations to understand mentally handicapped people.

3. 21 churches would like help in training people to work with the mentally handicapped.

4. 70 churches would like to know what material is available for working with mentally handicapped people in churches.

5. 64 churches would like suggestions as so how to support parents with mentally handicapped children.

2. Some Organizations Offering Support and Information

A Cause for Concern and *Causeway*
   PO Box 351, Reading, RG1 7AL
Information, education, help for churches, residential. Protestant.

Care Trust
   53 Romsey Street, London SW1P 3RF
Information, campaigning. Protestant.

L'Arche
   14 London Road, Beccles, Suffolk NR34 9NH
Help for churches, residential. Catholic.

Mencap
   123 Golden Lane, London EC1 0RT
General. Secular.